DRAFTEE MARCHES WITH THE
BAND OF BROTHERS

By Chris Langlois

Illustrated by Dawn Secord

ISBN: 979-8-9874897-3-4

Dedicated to the men who ran Currahee Mountain as a badge of honor.

Draftee was a real dog and his adventure was real. However, most of the barking dialogue was made up by the author...to present this story from a dog's point of view.

"...Don't be afraid to go into your library and read every book..."

Dwight D. Eisenhower, 5-star General in the United States Army, Supreme Commander of the Allied Expeditionary Forces during WWII and the 34th President of the United States.

UNITED STATES ARMY DURING WWII (4,000,000 MEN)

✪

101ST AIRBORNE DIVISION (12,000 MEN)

✪

506TH PARACHUTE INFANTRY REGIMENT (1,800 MEN)

✪

2ND BATTALION (600 MEN)

✪

EASY COMPANY (160 MEN)

✪

PLATOON (48 MEN)

✪

SQUAD (16 MEN)

I don't remember the first name I had, or if I ever really had a name. I never really had a home either.

The open road was where I slept and where I found my next meal.

But I'd always wished I had a warm place to sleep, a full belly...and someone to love me.

It was just another day, but then, I heard a noise!

It was very faint at first, and sounded like it was far away. I looked down the red dirt road, but I did not see anything.

Wait, what is that big cloud of dust?

All of a sudden, I saw some people. They were coming my way. But it wasn't just a couple of people. Oh no! It was a whole bunch of people and they just kept coming and coming.

I could feel the ground shaking with each step they took. How many of them were there?! The lines looked like they went on forever.

They were singing, "Don't sit under the apple tree with anyone else but me, anyone else but me, anyone else but me."

They came closer to me.

I thought they looked kinda funny. They didn't walk like regular people. They all walked in lines and in the same steps...left, right, left, right, left, right.

Almost every man carried a rifle. Some men carried a big, heavy rifle. Some men carried parts for that heavy gun. Some men carried a radio on their backs. Some men had a red cross on their arm and a bag of medical bandages.

They all wore the same clothes. And their clothes were the same color. That's boring.

I sat and watched them as they passed by. When they weren't singing, they were smiling and laughing.

Some were eating Hershey chocolate bars. Some were chewing bubble gum.

Left, right.
Left, right.
Left, right.

Many of them said, "Hi, puppy." as they passed by. A couple even reached down to pet me as they walked by. That made my tail wag!

They all had red dirt on their boots and on their pants. I guess they had been walking on this road for a long time.

I wondered where they were going. I wondered what was so important.

I kinda wanted to ask them those questions. So I said, "Bark, bark, bark."

"Hey look DeWitt, that dog seems to have a lot to tell you." said one of the men. The man named DeWitt stopped and knelt down to pet my head. The other men kept walking.

All of a sudden, a gruff voice shouted from behind, "Soldier, get back in formation!" DeWitt hurried to catch up and got back in line with his buddies.

But now I knew why the men were dressed the same and walked in lines, they were soldiers.

The soldiers continued walking away. But I sure did like when DeWitt scratched my head. It had been a long time since someone took the time to pet me. I had to catch up to DeWitt!Besides, they didn't answer my questions. What were they doing? Where were they going?

So I ran as fast as I could and though all the soldiers were wearing the same colored uniforms, I found DeWitt!

I showed him my trick of standing on my two back feet and he smiled down at me.

"Well," DeWitt said to me, "I guess you are determined to make this march to Atlanta with us, huh?"

I had never heard of Atlanta but I already liked DeWitt. Wherever he was going, I wanted to go too.

And again that same gruff voice yelled, "DeWitt, you better get up here in formation or you're gonna owe me push-ups!!"

A little while later, the men took a break from walking. They called what they were doing, marching.

"Hey DeWitt, whatcha gonna call him?" asked Bud.

Then the shouts started coming fast:
"How about Toccoa?"
"I like General Barker."
"What about Colonel?"
"We could call him Currahee!"

DeWitt looked down at me and smiled. "Draftee," he said so softly so that only I could hear him. That made me smile. Although I didn't know what it meant, I liked the sound of that name.

"Alright boys, y'all meet Draftee!" said DeWitt. All of the men around me cheered and shouted out, "Draftee!"

My tail wagged harder and faster than it ever had. Then they all scratched my head.

I finally had a name.

"Hey, DeWitt, don't you have enough to carry? Are you gonna carry Draftee all the way to Atlanta?" asked one of the soldiers.

"No sir, **we** are gonna carry Draftee all the way to Atlanta." DeWitt replied.

DeWitt moved some items around in his backpack and made room for me to be strapped in with his socks. Then we were off walking - I mean, marching - once again.

The soldiers talked about why they were marching. Apparently, their boss, Colonel Sink, wanted them to beat a world record. They had to get from their Army base at Camp Toccoa to the big city of Atlanta, Georgia. It was 118 miles away! There was no way I was going to be able to walk that far by myself.

But if someone else was going to do the marching, I was not going to complain... ridin' is better than walkin'.

After a while, we stopped for a break. The men looked tired. Some looked <u>really</u> tired. I could hear them all say their feet hurt. But still, they cracked jokes with each other. I could tell they had spent a lot of time together and were very good friends.

The men pulled food from their backpacks and drank water from their canteens. Each one threw some pieces of food my way. Boy was I glad, all that marching made me hungry!

Most of the men complained that Army food tasted terrible, but I thought it all tasted wonderful. It was certainly better than all the scraps I had been eating lately.

Then there was that same gruff voice yelling, "Alright Easy Company, we move out in five minutes!" Ah, so this whole group of soldiers was called Easy Company.

"Someone wake up Malarkey." said Skip.

I was too excited to sleep, but, I wasn't doing the marching.

At night, everyone finally got a chance to sleep in a field just off the road. Each soldier carried one half of a tent and together, two men made a small tent. It got cold at night but I stayed warm sleeping with my buddy DeWitt.

We had to wake up early the next morning. I ate some more Army food for breakfast and DeWitt strapped me in for the ride – um, I mean march.

But soon the clouds arrived...and then, so did the rain. The temperature dropped and the men weren't sweating anymore. We were wet and cold and tired. The soldiers' boots were muddy.

This march had been hard on all the soldiers. They weren't lucky to be carried like me. Some of the soldiers hurt their feet, ankles and legs on the wet and icy ground. Though hurt, they refused to quit or get into the ambulance that followed at the end of the group. Their buddies took turns holding them up so they could continue to march.

I thought they were very brave and very strong.

The last day, the rain stopped.

This was such a big event, a newspaper man came out to meet the soldiers and tell their story. He said he wanted to take a picture of me too. I'll be the most famous dog in all of Georgia!

As we got near the place everyone called Atlanta, it reminded me of when I first met Easy Company. There was a faint sound and I could see a lot of people. But this time, it was a crowd of regular people, not soldiers. They were all waving American flags and cheering for the soldiers. There was even a marching band playing.

The soldiers marched into town with their heads held high and with big smiles. I could see the soldiers were very proud. And I was doing my part by wagging my tail.

Easy Company had marched into Atlanta and reached their goal of breaking the world record!

The next day, we took a passenger train to Fort Benning. Now that was exciting! Why march when this train went so fast? I guess soldiers don't always take the easy way out.

The march to Atlanta was just a part Easy Company's Army training. I listened while the soldiers talked about why they were going to Fort Benning.

Now they were going to school to learn how to jump out of airplanes. Then a parachute on their back would gently float them to the ground? Well, that sounded like a crazy story to me. Only birds float in the air.

They said at the end of school, they would be called "paratroopers." That sounded like a pretty fancy job to me.

Once we arrived at Fort Benning, there was so much to see.

There were tall towers with soldiers attached to parachutes and, just as they had described on the train, the soldiers were floating to the ground.

There were soldiers running in groups in all directions.

I saw men climbing ropes for exercise.

We passed a hospital with a few nurses standing outside. They looked very different from the soldiers with their all-white dresses, hats and shoes. Each of the nurses wanted to pet me and I surely didn't mind that one bit.

"I wish we could keep him!" said one of the nurses. "I love him!" said another.

DeWitt looked down at me and smiled.

"Well Draftee, I have a lot of special training to do here. I think these nice ladies will be glad to take care of you from now on."

A nurse held me in her arms and said, "Don't you worry, he's in safe hands with us." My tail was wagging, but I also felt sad to see my friend leave.

DeWitt ran to catch up with his buddies - one last time.

I knew the soldiers had already been in Army training for a while and they had more tough training to do.

I felt like the march to Atlanta had been my first Army training. Now I was a real United States Army dog, Private Draftee!

As I waved my tail goodbye, I was already missing my buddy DeWitt and the soldiers who had become my friends. But I knew DeWitt and his buddies would soon be proud paratroopers.

As they marched away, the soldiers not only looked like a band of brothers, they also looked like heroes to me.

And for me, well, I finally found a home, a warm place to sleep, a full belly... and someone who loved me.

The March from Camp Toccoa to Atlanta

118 MILES IN 75 HOURS

ACTUAL MARCHING TIME WAS 33 HOURS, 30 MINUTES

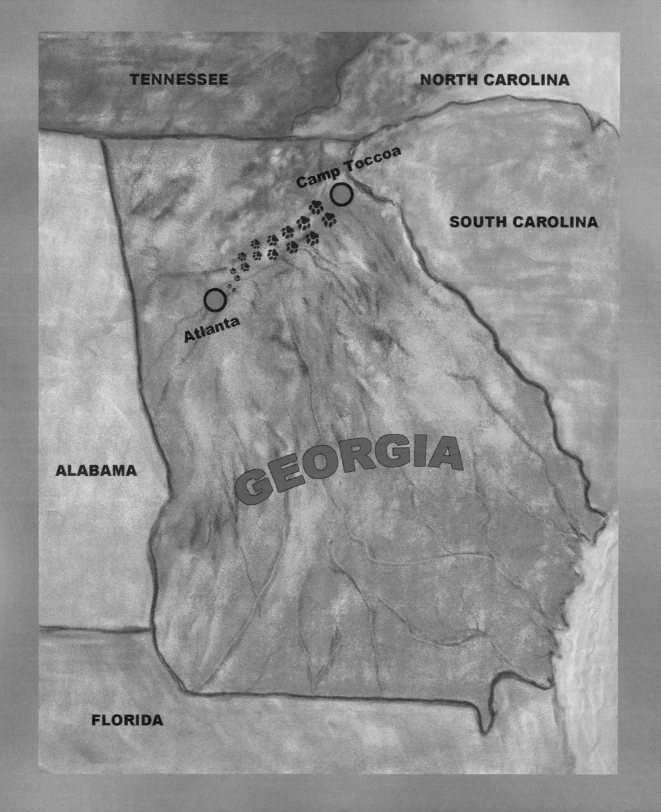

In November of 1942, Colonel Robert F. Sink, commander of the 506th Parachute Infantry Regiment of the 101st Airborne Division read a story in Reader's Digest magazine. The story described how Japanese Army soldiers completed a 100-mile march in record-setting time. They finished the march so quickly it broke a previous Guinness World Record.

Colonel Sink, knowing that his soldiers were in tip-top shape, decided that his men would break that newly established record. After all, the Japanese had attacked the United States at a place called Pearl Harbor, in December of 1941. That attack forced the United States into World War II. Colonel Sink wanted to show everyone that his men were better soldiers than the Japanese.

It was decided that the men of Colonel Sink's 2nd Battalion would break the record starting on the 1st of December, 1942; as they had trained the hardest of all the 506th at Camp Toccoa. The march was from Camp Toccoa, Georgia all the way to Atlanta, Georgia. The total distance was 118 miles…and it had to be done in three days!

The weather was perfect when the men started marching on December 1st. But the sun soon hid behind the clouds, and rain and sleet started to fall. Despite the fast-paced marching, the men were soon soaking wet. They grumbled all day about the heavy weight of their weapons, and of being wet and cold. Finally, they stopped for the night, sleeping in small tents at the side of the road.

The next day the weather cleared up. It was still cloudy but at least it didn't rain on them. As the men continued marching, they noticed they had company…a small dog started tagging along. One of the men, DeWitt Lowery from Alabama, smiled as the little dog, all white with brown spots around its head, tried to keep up with the fast-marching soldiers.

DeWitt liked the dog right away. He was tough and didn't quit, kind of like the soldiers he ran alongside of during the march. DeWitt liked him so much, he gave him the name, "Draftee."

A reporter had come along for the march to write a story for his newspaper and when he saw Draftee with DeWitt, he started to get his camera out. The other soldiers began kidding DeWitt, calling him by his nickname, "Alabama." "Look, Alabama's trying to get a movie contract." called out a fellow from South Philadelphia by the name of Bill Guarnere.

As the soldiers took a break, DeWitt noticed that Draftee had been limping. It was obvious his paws were hurting from trying to keep up with the march. Not wanting to see the puppy hurting, DeWitt took out a pair of socks and used them to strap Draftee to his pack. Now Draftee was riding instead of walking, and doing it in style. The reporter saw DeWitt carrying Draftee and took a picture. The photo ended up being one of the most popular in the reporter's newspaper.

That evening, when the men put up their tents, Draftee stayed with DeWitt, snuggled up next to him for warmth. When they got up in the morning, DeWitt used his socks again to strap Draftee to his pack. He rode the rest of the way in style, eating Army rations fed to him by all of DeWitt's buddies.

As the long line of soldiers marched into Atlanta, the city turned out to see the men complete a new world record. It became a parade, with a marching band and cheering people lining Peachtree Street. When the music started Draftee's ears perked up and he seemed to enjoy the parade as much as the soldiers. They marched through town and put up their tents in a small field and just like the night before, Draftee stayed with DeWitt.

Per Stephen Ambrose's book, Band of Brothers, 586 soldiers began the march and only 12 failed to finish. A true testament to their toughness and determination to not fail Col. Sink and their brothers marching beside them.

The next day, the men climbed aboard a train destined for Fort Benning, Georgia where they would take their paratrooper training, learning to jump from a C-47 airplane and land using parachutes. And do you know who was on the train with them? That's right…Draftee!

Because they had worked so hard on the march, after arriving at Fort Benning, the soldiers were given three days off to enjoy themselves. Knowing he couldn't keep Draftee, DeWitt found a group of Army nurses who were looking for a pet. When he brought Draftee to them, they quickly fell in love with the friendly little puppy. Draftee had made a world-record march, found a bunch of new friends, and now, had a new home where he would be well taken care of.

It was quite an adventure for a little stray dog from the fields of Georgia!

CHRIS LANGLOIS is a grandson of medic Eugene Gilbert Roe, Sr. "Doc" Roe joined Easy Company at Camp Mackall, just after Camp Toccoa, and was the only medic in Easy Company to make the jumps on D-Day and in Holland, to endure the cold of the Battle of the Bulge and to reach the Eagle's Nest at the war's end. Easy Company was made world-famous by the HBO miniseries Band of Brothers.

Chris is originally from Baton Rouge, Louisiana and graduated from Louisiana State University. He resides in Dallas, Texas with his daughter, Julia. Chris is a police officer on the streets in Dallas where he enjoys meeting new people and placing them in jail.

Chris' first book, *How Easy Company Became a Band of Brothers* has reached over 23 countries outside the United States and has been translated into French, Dutch, German and Chinese. His second book, *Patrick the Paratrooper,* like *Draftee,* is also meant to 'reach and teach' early readers as a way to introduce our WWII heroes. Chris can be reached at docroegrandson@gmail.com and on Facebook and Instagram under Doc Roe Publishing.

DAWN SECORD was raised in Texas and enjoys spending time with her dogs, cats, horses and critters. When not outside, she is inside drawing and painting animals or reading. In 1996, she left the corporate world to pursue a career as a fine artist. Her favorite mediums are oil and pastel.

Dawn's paintings have won many awards and have been featured on magazine covers and as featured stories in national art, business and animal publications.

Dawn has illustrated children's books as well as historical books. She wrote and illustrated *No Ghoulish Green Monsters Here,* which features her dog as the main character. She also shows her dogs competitively.

Dawn lives in Texas with her husband on a hobby farm with their rollicking Irish Setters, some pampered cats, a lively cockatiel, a small flock of awesome fluffy chickens and a rooster named Fabio. She can be reached at www.dawnsecord.com